Work In Progress

A rainbow of emotions

Sneha Deshpande Vaidya

BookLeaf Publishing

India | USA | UK

Dedication

This book is dedicated to my parents Sunil and Chitra, my sisters, Swapna and Shweta, who first encouraged me to share my word. To my husband Amit, who has always supported me through thick and thin.And finally to my readers, who find a part of themselves within these pages.

Thank you.

Preface

Work in Progress is a collection of short poems, written across the various stages of my life.

I write to capture the tapestry of human experience: the joy of creating memories, the thrill of falling in love, the pain of heartbreak and the resilience of regrowth, the lessons learned from hard truths and life's challenges - the journey towards becoming a complete person.

It's about embracing the full spectrum of emotions that life has to offer - **A rainbow of emotions**.

Acknowledgements

This book would not exist without the unwavering support of my family and friends.
Thank you for your patience, your encouragement, and your belief in me.

1. Evenings in Bali

Flowy dresses and messy tresses
A cool breeze that gently caresses
Cane lanterns and rattan ceilings
Cocktails, beach clubs and balmy evenings
Perfect water to float or splash a friend
Loud music to dance till your heart's content
Conversations that last till 3 a.m.
& in 4 hours, ready to do it all again
Tunes that remind me of another time
another life, another place, brings a smile
We made memories to last a lifetime!

2. Memories

I thought life is for creating wonderful memories
Chase dreams and create legacies
Experience the northern lights,
walk on the ocean floor, crawling through the caves,
inhale the icy glaciers, the vast mountains
stroll across beaches, hiking valleys,
get splashed in the waterfalls, the rivers, the lakes
visit the unknown, experience life as they say
do something important, leave the world a better place
Must make memories every single day!
But sometimes I wonder,
If 3 generations on, I might not exist,
and what if tomorrow I forget your face,
a cherished relationship gone without a trace
what then is this life's memories worth,
What then are these memories' purpose?

3. I'm Your Friend

You can run to me
When your spirits are low
When a friend turns into a foe
When your day seems bad
Or when you are just feeling sad
You can come to me
When life is a mess
When you rip your favourite dress
When you think you can't stand it anymore
or when you have needles in your heart's core
You know I'm there for you
When you break up with your boyfriend
When liabilities makes you tense
When you think you have no one
Think of me, I'm always there, I'm your friend.

4. This is Love I'm sure

Beneath a thousand stars
Atop a carpet of grass
You and me lie awake
Until dawn breaks
The cruel demon of loneliness
Has parted with the dusk
Heaven has embraced us
Filled us with love, happiness and trust
A tranquil aura to treasure
Surrounds us like a shield
Emits a fragrance so pure
This is love, I'm sure.

5. Love that I never got

You know I love you, 'coz I've told you so
You know I'll do anything for you when your spirits are
low
I've told you time and time again
I won't leave you, whether there is sunshine or rain
No answer I've got till this day
Waiting for you, will wait till my hair is grey
I feel your kindness in every way
If you love me, why not say?
I may not be the one in your life
I may not be the light that you seek
If I am, then ask me , "will you be mine?"
If not then with my sorrows and grief leave me behind
Time is a healer and I'll smile again
In my heart there might be some pain
You might even forget me but I will not
You are the love that I never got

6. Unknown Feelings

One moment close, the other apart
Our bond a mystery, unknown by far
What's in your mind, what do you feel?
Mine's a blur, a tangled reel
Highs and lows come and go
My feelings I don't want to show
Not unless I know for sure
That what we share is something forever, something
pure
Who will make the first move and what will it be
Will it be confident and transparent for everyone to see?
Right now my cup is full and I fear
Of the unknown feelings about to appear

7. Time

It's that time now
when I have to leave
The time for me to see
the truth behind the scene
The time for letting go
all my favourite memories
The time to get over
all the pain and worries
The time to understand
that no longer you are mine
The time to realise
We've left love far behind
The time to open my eyes
and see we've chosen different ways
The time to learn
that we are at a point of no return
The time has come

8. Reborn

Baby since you've gone
My wish to live has reborn
I never believed it would feel so good
I'm glad I've done what I should
In life one has relationships so many
Our own from time to time has varied
Friendship, love and dislike we shared
Although both of us for each other cared
Though parting at first gave pain
Slowly I realised what I've gained
The time spent with you felt cold-hearted
I don't regret that we met or that we parted
Happy we both are with the present state
I guess for each other we were never made

9. Nights

Driving through the traffic
A journey never ending
Can't wait till I reach home
These headlights are blinding
As the night falls
Feelings of stress depart
I wanna dance, be myself
Now my day, my time really starts
Responsibilities need to be fulfilled
For that I give my day
But as the night approaches
I party my gloom away
As the dawn arrives
A new rat race has begun
Can't wait till I'm free again
Can't wait for the night to drown the sun

10. My Mother

A burst of laughter when least expected
A grin or coquettish look when teased
The haste to remove specs before a click
An ask to check if she was still thin!
A need for speed in everything
But reckless motorists be aware
Drive safely when around her
or Ghadhe ka baccha will be yelled !
Lipsticks, compact and kajal
was all she needed to look so great
if you sat beside her on the couch
Expectations to massage her hands will be made !
Never stopped celebrating be the news big or small
Complimented others, learnt from all
Told us to put 100% effort, whatever the outcome
To be true to yourself and sleep with a clear conscience
Feminist, leader and way ahead of the times
Had a joyful glee be it diamonds or ice cream
Filled every event with joy and laughter
The apple of everyone's eye, I present my mother!

11. I Miss You!

I miss you in the mornings
I miss you at night
I forget you are not around sometimes
And when I remember I wish to hug you tight
I miss you in the shower
Or when I'm sitting alone
I remember the fun times we had
And wish we had more
I miss your voice and I miss your smile
I miss fighting with you and getting annoyed
I miss the moments we shared
I miss your advice
But whenever I think of you, I laugh
At all the fun times we had
all the amazing memories we shared
And the laugh turns into a cry
I miss you a lot, every moment, I miss you mom !

12. A New Date

Suddenly there is a new date in our lives
one that wasn't envisioned nor was it hoped
it wasn't asked for, it was told
It came and now it will stay forever
it can't be erased,
a date that will be forgotten never
So I play the music loud
To drown the cry from within
Beats that pump and surround
To hide the heart shattering
The sky it has lost its blue
The water, it's not as cool
A shivering comes from deep inside
a wave of apathy rolls beside
When everything is lost and we seek hope
with this new date, how will we cope ?

13. Lost a Parent Club

When things are tough, I need you beside me
When things are great, with you I want to celebrate
When it gets serious, I remember your laughter
and sometimes when I dress up, I can see you in the
mirror
When I'm lonely, only you know how I feel
When I'm angry, I need you to say, "it's not a big deal"
I've been added to the "lost a parent" club,
an unwanted lifelong membership, so cruel so
permanent
Moving on and missing less?
The experienced know that's just a dream
Life has changed, a constant vacuum created
Never will anything be the same again...

14. Changes

No matter what you think of the past
No matter what grudge you hold
The future will your change your mind one day
And bring happiness and love in a fold
Coz for every sad moment in your life
There's a good happy one in the corner
You just have to open your heart and seek
Not close your eyes with a tear underneath
I've often wondered how time can heal
And what it can do to what I feel
But I've realised it's true what they say
Time can and does change the way
As everything changes, it changes every day
So what you thought was true, isn't there any more
Neither the sadness nor the joy
They are just fleeting memories
It's up to you how to react and what you want to do

15. Strength

When the need arises
We can pack our life in boxes
Leave a world we built behind
Travel a million miles
When the need arises
We can find the energy to complete
A task that's been waiting for eternity
Finished it like it was all just too easy
When the need arises
We can find the strength to cope
With life's winding speed bumps
That can shift and throw you off course
When the need arises
Strength from within is found
It was always there, you had it in you
Now it's out and so is a new stronger you!

16. Trust

Bit by bit you lost my trust
Saying one and doing another
Just under radar, just barely legal
Bit by bit you lost my trust
Conspiring behind doors,
causing swirls, unrequired distractions, chaos
Bit by bit you lost my trust
You ask, and ask, but never share, never tell
Hide information like its power, hindering is your
armour
Bit by bit you lost my trust
"Oops I'm sorry but it's done", excuses given
Pretends to collaborate, but with selfish motives
Bit by bit you lost my trust
Once twice and thrice again
Trusted you and got drenched in the acid rain

17. Identity

What's in a name they say
She replies, my identity, my reflection, my
perceptions,me
What's in a face they say
She responds, my memories, my smile, my emotions, me
What's in relationship they say
She fights my love, my soul, my partner, me
What's in this life, they say
A short journey, each moment unique, stories untold, my
world.

18. Greed

With so many natural disasters and diseases taking
human life,
How can we as a human race justify killings
for reasons man made, for borders we create
for power and pleasure, for money without measure?

What is the cost of an arm, a leg ,
a wife, a dad, a son, a bed,
of a house, a school and medical needs,
What is the cost of human greed ?

19. Caged

Under the weight of expectations
Life is lived in moderation
An invisible cage surrounds
Restricting from reaching heights
Stopping from freeing flights
Once in a while the gate opens
To a far away place, always close to nature
Heart is full, Cup is filled,
And then back to the treadmill
A fog of darkness bringing me down
Pulling me in, keeping me bound
No strength to get up, can't be bothered
Let me lay here, roll in this forever
And then sparks a friendly conversation
A curved voice of reason tries to get through
Show me how much I am valued,
See how great the need, the love, is the plead
& for a mere moment I'm back but knowing deep inside
that the fog is rolling just beyond waiting to meet again
Trap me in the cage, in the den.

20. Colours

Blue, Orange, Pink and Grey
Colours that change through the day
mirroring my highs and my lows
Oh beautiful sky, in your arms my mood you hold

Sap, Teal, Sage and Olive
Rustling movements, active yet passive
Greens of the forest that capture my emotions
Grooving with soft, unseen connections

White, Turquoise or milky Beige
frothing, bubbling, or still like a calming blank page
Sea, you talk to me in different ways
Uplifting yet quiet, drenching me in your sprays

Maroon, Red, Brown and Ocher Gold
With the heat you give, you make me bold
Your gravity, your power, you control me, own me,
Mother earth in your warmth, is where I'm meant to be

21. Forever it shall last

Once more the rain pours
Once more I sit by the window sill while the wind roars
Once more I remember the past
The love we shared, forever it shall last
Once more I take a walk by water
Once more I'm reminded of how we planned our future
in the wander
Once more I remember the past
The love we shared, forever it shall last
Once more I'm in the car
Once more flashes the accident that made you go far
Once more I remember the past
The love we shared, forever it shall last
Once more I'm sobbing while it rains
Once more I cry out in pain
Once more I remember the past
The love we shared, forever it shall last

9 789367 390825